Postcards of **Political Icons**

Postcards of

Political Icons

Leaders of the Twentieth Century

Introduction by
Andrew Roberts

Bodleian Library
UNIVERSITY OF OXFORD

The Bodleian Library would like to thank John Fraser, John Pinfold, and Dr Anne Deighton for their assistance in producing this book.

First published in 2008 by the Bodleian Library
Broad Street
Oxford OX1 3BG

www.bodleianbookshop.co.uk

ISBN 13: 978 1 85124 327 3

Introduction © Andrew Roberts, 2008
This edition © Bodleian Library, University of Oxford, 2008

The John Fraser Collection of Propaganda Postcards is part of the John Johnson Collection of Printed Ephemera in the Bodleian Library.

Designed by Dot Little
Printed in Slovenia by Impress dd
British Library Catalogue in Publishing Data
A CIP record of this publication is available from the British Library

Collector's Foreword

From an early age I was interested in history. My mother gave me my first postcard, of King George VI at his coronation. When she took me to St Paul's Cathedral, I bought a postcard of Nelson's statue. In 1944 my local Woolworths sold sepia photographic postcards of generals Eisenhower, Alexander, and Montgomery. From then on I was a compulsive collector of any postcards of a historical or current political interest.

I was strongly influenced by the example of my artist aunt, Helen McKie (pronounced to rhyme with key). She had a large collection of postcards, mainly of views, arranged in order of country and subject matter, which she used for reference purposes. So I had her example to follow, and after her death I acquired her postcards of Hitler (she was the first woman artist to be allowed in the Brown House when she was commissioned to do a series on Germany in 1932 for the *Sketch*) and also cards of Rome with its Fascist décor. (There is an entry for her in *Who Was Who* for the 1950s.)

John Fraser, London

Introduction

What makes an iconic photograph? What are the attributes of an image that can convey the *idea* of a political leader, as well as just their physical features? How have politicians manipulated the photographic art in order to try to create their own cult of the personality, and why have some succeeded while others manifestly failed? These are a few of the questions we should ask ourselves when reading this superb collection of postcards of political icons from the twentieth century.

Most of the postcards from which this collection is taken were amassed over a lifetime by John Fraser, one of the greatest of all the British postcard collectors, and generously donated to the Bodleian Library in Oxford. (A small number not from the collection are here included for the sake of completeness.) Together they comprise a truly comprehensive view of modern political iconography, from which certain broad lessons can, I believe, be learnt.

The first is that quite as much as actors and magicians, politicians need props. This stemmed from the days before high-definition photography and the moving image, when caricature and newspaper sketches showed the public what their statesmen looked like. In order to differentiate themselves to the electorate, therefore, Gladstone wore an unfeasibly high collar, Lord Randolph Churchill a handlebar moustache, Joseph Chamberlain regularly sported an orchid in his buttonhole, and so on.

As is clear from these postcards, the prop survived and prospered in the twentieth century: where would Lord Randolph's son Winston Churchill be without his bow-tie and V-for-victory sign, Yasser Arafat without his kefiyah, Charles de Gaulle without his kepi and cigarette, Ho Chi Minh without his long straggly beard, or Che Guevara without his cigar? Whether they were sported deliberately or not – and they mostly were – props became associated with the politician in the public imagination. Small wonder the CIA attempted to feed Fidel Castro poisons that would make his beard fall out, thus denuding him of a potent political asset.

Very often when it came to medals and decorations, less was more when trying to emphasize the (often feigned) modesty of the sitter in a posed photograph. Thus although Field-Marshal Hindenburg had in fact been awarded almost every Prussian order and decoration going, he sits wearing only the single ribbon of the Iron Cross. He nonetheless looks far more regal than Emperor Hirohito of Japan, with his chest full of medals and stars which seem utterly redundant on the breast of someone whose subjects, after all, claimed he was a living god.

Where decorations can be used to signal effect is in establishing precedence over people who are similarly dressed. The photo of President Anwar Sadat sitting next to his lieutenant Hosni Mubarak at a grand parade is notable for the number of subtle sartorial ways in which Sadat is shown to be in charge. Note how the braid on Mubarak's peaked hat is silver, whereas Sadat's otherwise identical hat is in gold; how Sadat has eight rows of medals to Mubarak's seven; how Mubarak's collar badge is grand, but Sadat's grander still, and how even Sadat's belt-buckle denotes a superior rank. These laughing neighbours are confidants and comrades-in-arms, the photo states, but Sadat is undoubtedly the superior.

By contrast Adolf Hitler never wore epaulettes or orders and decorations, barring the Iron Cross medal and badge he was awarded for being wounded in the Great War. He wanted to pose as the 'ordinary German' whom Fate had raised up to avenge the humiliations of 1918. In the photo here he is dressed in a natty civilian suit with one-inch pin stripes, a microscopic tie knot, and big turn-ups, looking for all the world like an eager middle-manager. It is chilling to think that if this photo was taken in the early 1930s, as seems likely, the unimpressed young Aryan lad in lederhosen being clasped – slightly unwillingly from his averted head – by the Führer would have been easily old enough to be killed in the war by 1945.

The only person to understand the cult of the personality better than Hitler in the twentieth century was Joseph Stalin, and the photo of him sharing a private joke with V.I. Lenin in this collection is easily as disconcerting as the one of the Führer with his unsuspecting future victim. Taken shortly before Lenin's death, when he was convalescing from an assassination attempt, the two men appear happy and relaxed – even confidential – in each other's company. In fact at that time Lenin was actively plotting to try to exclude Stalin from power after his own demise, and Stalin was hoping Lenin would die before that could happen. Yet they look at the camera with a shared smile, as though they knew the photographer was about to be purged as soon as the negatives were developed.

Here is Kaiser Wilhelm II of Germany, too, haughtily staring into the lens, the Grand Cross of the military order of the Pour la Mérite ('the Blue Max') at his throat, his withered hand hidden from sight, and a sword hanging at the side of his be-strapped boots. It was once said of a portrait of him that it was 'not so much a painting as a declaration of war', and the same is true of this photo.

Although Prussian hauteur precluded the Kaiser and Hindenburg from smiling, as the twentieth century progressed smiles became almost de rigueur for politicians, especially in the democratic West. The huge, full-face, perfectly-teethed smiles on the faces of the three Kennedy brothers exude confidence in the future; it is only we who know how tragic life was to turn out for the eldest two. Smiles can be a conjuror's trick; look at the grin on the face of cuddly, lovable Chairman Mao as he sits in his simple wicker chair in a rural setting on the Yangtze. Yet many claim he was responsible for the deaths of seventy million Chinese.

Look at Kemal Atatürk's eyebrows drawn to resemble the wings of an eagle in flight. Or Eva Perón's carefully braided blonde hair and lovely smile. With this fine collection as our guide, we should not fall for such obvious tricks of political image manipulation ever again. Yet we doubtless will.

Andrew Roberts

The Postcards

Kaiser Wilhelm II (1859–1941)

Queen Victoria's eldest grandchild, the Kaiser was born with a withered left arm and deaf in his right ear. He was also often said to be 'not quite normal' and may have suffered brain damage at birth. Regarded by many as vain and bombastic, he was happiest when surrounded by the military and had a great love of uniforms and military display. He succeeded his father as German Emperor in 1888, and two years later engineered the resignation of Bismarck, with the intention of ruling as an absolute monarch. During the next twenty-five years, leading up to the First World War, he managed to alienate all of the other European powers with the exception of Austria-Hungary. His attempts to find Germany 'a place in the sun' and to build up the Imperial German Navy alarmed Britain, with whom the Kaiser had a love–hate relationship all his life. Opinion remains divided on the extent to which he was responsible for the outbreak of the First World War, but it seems that, whilst he had no desire for a general European war, he did nothing to rein in the militarists in his own country and sanctioned the Austrians in their desire to use force against Serbia. Once war broke out, the supposedly all-powerful Kaiser became increasingly impotent as the generals took over the direction of Germany. In the autumn of 1918 the Kaiser, faced with mutinies in both the army and the navy, and with the possibility of revolution in Berlin, abdicated just two days before the Armistice. Later some historians have suggested he subscribed to the legend of the 'stab in the back', and blamed the Jews for his abdication. He fled to Holland and spent the rest of his life in exile there.

Kaiser Wilhelm II.
im Jagdanzuge.

Original-Aufnahme v.
Selle & Kuntze-Niederastroth,
Königl. Hofphotographen in Potsdam.

3632
Verlag von Gustav Liersch & Co.
BERLIN S.W.

POST CARD.

THE ADDRESS ONLY TO BE
WRITTEN HERE

ROTARY PHOTOGRAPHIC SERIES

Nicholas II (1868–1918)

Emperor and Autocrat of all the Russias, to give him his official title, Nicholas succeeded his father as Tsar in 1894. He had little of the strength of character of his father, Alexander III, but was nevertheless determined to maintain Russia as an absolute monarchy. In 1895 he declared that those who sought greater democracy in Russia were pursuing 'senseless dreams'. However, following defeat in the Russo-Japanese war of 1904–05, and the first Russian Revolution of 1905, he was forced to offer concessions and to agree to the establishment of a parliament, the Duma. By 1906 the forces of autocracy had largely regained control of the country and the powers of the Duma were reduced. Despite ongoing revolutionary activity, Nicholas might nevertheless have retained power had he not led Russia into the First World War. Military defeats at the front were compounded by government inefficiency and corruption. In September 1915 Nicholas took personal command of the army, thus linking himself directly to its military failures, whilst at the same time removing himself from St Petersburg so that he was unaware of the extent of popular unrest in the capital. By February 1917 he had lost the confidence of both the politicians and the generals and was forced to abdicate. Following the abdication, the royal family were initially imprisoned at Tsarskoye Selo, but were later moved first to Tobolsk and then to Ekaterinburg where they were murdered by local Bolsheviks in July 1918. The circumstances of his death made Nicholas into a martyr for some people, and whereas he was known as 'Bloody Nicholas' during his lifetime, he is now officially 'St Nicholas the Passion Bearer' to the Russian Orthodox Church.

CZAR NICHOLAS OF RUSSIA.

18 B

13

Emmeline Pankhurst (1858–1928)

Mrs Pankhurst was the leading figure in the British suffragette movement in the years leading up to the First World War. Born in Manchester into a family with radical tendencies, in 1879 she married the socialist Richard Pankhurst. In 1889 she formed the Women's Franchise League with the aim of obtaining the vote for women in local elections, and in 1903 she founded the Women's Social and Political Union, which became the leading suffragette organization. The WSPU became famous for its militancy, and Mrs Pankhurst was herself arrested on several occasions and force-fed in prison after going on hunger strike. At the beginning of the First World War she suspended the suffragette campaign, arguing that support of the war effort should come first, and that women should take over men's jobs, enabling them to join up. This strategy may have played its part in leading to the Representation of the People Act of 1918, which for the first time gave votes to women, although only to those over thirty and possessing some property rights. Mrs Pankhurst was an autocratic leader who split with other suffragettes, including her daughter Sylvia Pankhurst, over the future direction of the movement. She gradually lost her socialist beliefs, and by the time of her death had been adopted as a prospective parliamentary candidate by the Conservative Party.

Mrs PANKHURST

BY Lena Connell
Balcom Rd Road

copyright

15

Paul von Hindenburg (1847–1934)

The epitome of the Prussian officer class, Hindenburg became military leader of Germany during the First World War, and later served as President of the Weimar Republic. As a young man he fought in Bismarck's wars against Austria (1866) and France (1870–1), and was present at the battles of Königgrätz and Sedan. He retired from the army in 1910, but was recalled at the beginning of the First World War and secured the overwhelming defeat of the Russians at the battle of Tannenberg. Further victories on the Eastern Front consolidated his prestige, and in 1916 he, together with Ludendorff, achieved not just the supreme direction of the German army but also increasingly of the civil government. Even in the defeat of 1918 Hindenburg remained a hero in Germany, and he may have contributed to the legend that Germany had not been militarily defeated but had succumbed to 'a stab in the back'. In 1925 he was persuaded to stand in the conservative interest as President of the Weimar Republic, an act for which he had first to ask the ex-Kaiser to release him from his oath of loyalty. He saw himself as an 'Ersatzkaiser' and carried out his constitutional duties with impeccable propriety. Re-elected in 1932, his last years in office were troubled, and his record was sullied by the role he played in supporting the Nazi seizure of power and the appointment of Hitler as Chancellor in 1933. Sir John Wheeler-Bennett characterized him as a 'Wooden Titan', impressive on the outside but hollow and empty within.

Generalfeldmarschall
von Hindenburg

Robert Fendius, Königl. Hof- und Kammerphotograph, Magdeburg.

17

POST CARD.

David Lloyd George (1863–1945)

Memorably described by J.M. Keynes as 'a half human visitor to our age from the hag ridden magic and enchanted woods of Celtic antiquity', Lloyd George was British Prime Minister from 1916 to 1922, when he was widely regarded, not least by himself, as the driving force behind Britain's victory in the First World War. Although born in Manchester, the 'Welsh Wizard' was brought up in Wales, and became Liberal M.P. for Caernarfon Boroughs in 1890. On the radical wing of the Liberal Party, he first came to prominence as a vocal opponent of the Anglo-Boer war of 1899–1902. When the Liberals returned to power in 1905 he was appointed President of the Board of Trade, becoming Chancellor of the Exchequer three years later. In this position he was largely responsible for the introduction of old age pensions, unemployment benefit and state financial support for the sick and infirm. To pay for these he introduced the 'People's Budget', which was rejected by the House of Lords and led to a Parliament Act, which considerably reduced the power of the unelected chamber. Considered a pacifist before 1914, he became the most outspoken proponent of fighting for total victory in the First World War. A parliamentary coup brought him to power in 1916 as leader of a coalition government. A raft of measures, including conscription, food rationing and liquor control were brought in and British industry was reorganized to make war production the top priority. Considered the architect of victory, Lloyd George won the 'Coupon Election' of 1918 on the promise to make Britain 'a land fit for heroes', but by 1922 his government had lost its lustre, being tarnished by the sale of honours at home and adventurism abroad. The Conservatives withdrew from the coalition and Lloyd George never held office again.

Mr LLOYD GEORGE.
AT HIS DESK.

copyright photo.
by E. H. MILLS.

Georges Clemenceau (1841–1929)

Known as 'Le Tigre', Clemenceau was Prime Minister of France from 1917 to 1920, during which time, in Churchill's vivid phrase: 'The truth is that Clemenceau embodied and expressed France. As much as any single human being, miraculously magnified, can ever be a nation, he was France.' As a young man he studied to become a physician, and he practised as a doctor in Montmartre. He was in Paris throughout the siege during the Franco-Prussian War, and later, as a radical member of the National Assembly, voted against the peace treaty with Germany. In 1876 he became a member of the Chamber of Deputies and in 1880 founded the radical newspaper *La Justice*. He gradually became known as a formidable political critic and as someone who could destroy governments, whilst being reluctant to take office himself. Anti-clerical, anti-monarchist, anti-German, anti-Communist, he was against tyranny in all its forms. Nevertheless, when Prime Minister in 1907–1910, he did not hesitate to order the suppression of popular strikes. He returned to power at the darkest period of the First World War, announcing 'We present ourselves before you with the single thought of total war.' An implacable opponent of Germany, he set himself against any leniency towards his defeated foe at the peace conference, arguing not just for the return of the lost French provinces of Alsace-Lorraine, but for a permanent French occupation of the Saarland and the transfer of German industry to France to compensate for France's losses during the war. The British and the Americans refused to support all of the French claims and Clemenceau was voted out of office in 1920 as a result. His memoirs, entitled *Grandeurs et misères d'une victoire*, contain the remarkable prediction that a future war with Germany was entirely possible and that 1940 would be the year of gravest danger.

Photo H. Martinie. Paris.

GEORGES CLEMENCEAU

DONT VIENNENT D'ÊTRE PUBLIÉS LES MÉMOIRES

GRANDEURS ET MISÈRES D'UNE VICTOIRE

Woodrow Wilson (1858–1924)

The twenty-eighth President of the United States, Wilson served two terms from 1912 to 1920. Before entering politics, Wilson was a political scientist, whose books *Congressional Government* and *Constitutional Government of the United States* explain much of his political thought. Although favourable towards a parliamentary form of government, Wilson accepted that the presidency 'will be as big and as influential as the man who occupies it'. Having been appointed President of Princeton University in 1902, Wilson entered politics and was elected Governor of New Jersey in 1910. Two years later he was elected as the first Democratic President of the USA since Grover Cleveland. His first term saw the successful implementation of many of his policies, based on the doctrine of the 'New Freedom'; these included anti-trust legislation, tariff reform, and reform of the banking system with the establishment of the Federal Reserve. Having been re-elected in 1916 as 'the man who kept us out of the war', Wilson spent most of his second term dealing with international affairs. He saw the First World War as 'a war to end war'. He formulated the Fourteen Points as a basis for a long-term peace, and argued for the establishment of a League of Nations to regulate international affairs. One of the 'big three', along with Clemenceau and Lloyd George, at the Paris peace conference at the end of the war, he was able to achieve the implementation of only four of the Fourteen Points in Europe, and although the League of Nations was established in Geneva, the US Senate blocked American participation in it. In 1919 Wilson was awarded the Nobel Peace Prize but suffered a stroke the same year. Nevertheless his principles of self-determination, collective security, democratic government, and the rule of international law, set the agenda for much of the rest of the twentieth century.

PRESIDENT WOODROW WILSON.   ROTARY PHOTO E.C.

9591 A

23

T.E. Lawrence (1888–1935)

Not least because of the magnificent David Lean film, *Lawrence of Arabia*, Lawrence remains an enigmatic figure of intense fascination, who, in Churchill's words, possessed 'that touch of genius which everyone recognizes and no-one can define'. Flamboyant, yet at the same time self-effacing, he was an archaeologist and a scholar who was also an undercover agent and a guerrilla leader. Having worked and travelled in the Ottoman Empire for many years before the First World War, he was the natural choice of the British authorities to incite the Arabs to revolt against their Turkish overlords. By adopting their dress and identifying himself with their cause, he succeeded in winning the Arabs to the Allied side and then conducted an effective campaign of guerrilla warfare along the Hejaz railway, which eventually led to the capture of Damascus. Lawrence believed that the Arabs should receive self-government after the war, and he pleaded their cause at the peace conference in Paris, but to little effect, as Britain and France carved up the territories of the former Ottoman Empire into spheres of influence. Lawrence proposed a very different set of boundaries to those which were adopted, his being based more on ethnic groups and commercial routes. After the war, Lawrence enlisted in the RAF under an assumed name and also served for a time in the Royal Tank Corps. He died in a motorcycle accident in 1935.

Vladimir Ilich Lenin (1870–1924) and Joseph Stalin (1879–1953)

Determined and ruthless, Lenin (left) was a professional revolutionary who not only developed Marxist thought to provide the Bolsheviks and Communists with their ideology, but was a superb tactician who masterminded the October 1917 Revolution that brought the Bolsheviks to power in Russia. No democrat, he then dissolved the Constituent Assembly once it became clear the Bolsheviks would not have a majority in it, proclaimed the dictatorship of the proletariat, and abrogated the will of the people to himself and his party. Highly effective in overcoming opposition, Lenin nevertheless showed a certain degree of pragmatism in his policies, adopting the more liberal New Economic Policy when the harsh measures of War Communism proved unpopular. Lenin was also opposed to personality cults and encouraged genuine debate within the party; both trends would be reversed after his untimely death.

Feared and revered in almost equal measure, Stalin (right) was the ultimate beneficiary of the Bolshevik Revolution. His years in the revolutionary underground made him keep his own counsel, and he was also a consummate actor, capable of playing many parts: Lenin's 'best pupil', the defender of socialist purity against deviationists and wreckers, the all-wise leader of his country, the Generalissimo who won the Second World War, and the all-powerful boss of the Communist Party. One of his strengths was to understand that power could be achieved by control of the bureaucracy, and he easily outmanoeuvred his rivals to achieve an unassailable position as dictator of the Soviet Union. Forced collectivization of agriculture and the purges of the 'Great Terror' caused untold suffering, but, despite initially failing to recognize the threat posed by Hitler, Stalin then led the USSR to victory in the 'Great Patriotic War' and made his country into a superpower.

Leon Trotsky (1879–1940)

Together with Lenin, Trotsky played a leading role in
the Bolshevik Revolution in Russia in 1917. Born into a
wealthy Ukrainian Jewish family, he first became involved
in revolutionary politics in 1896. Arrested in 1898, he
was exiled to Siberia, but escaped and joined Lenin in
London in 1902. He attended the second conference of
the Russian Social Democratic Labour Party in 1903, at
which time he was associated with the Mensheviks rather
than Lenin's Bolsheviks. Later he described himself as a
'non-factional social democrat', and began to develop
his theory of 'permanent revolution'. In 1905, during
the first Russian Revolution, Trotsky returned to Russia
and organized the first soviet in St Petersburg. By the
end of the year he was widely seen as the leader of the
Revolution, and, following its failure, he was again exiled to
Siberia, and again escaped. When the February Revolution
broke out in 1917 he immediately returned to Russia and
by the time of the October Revolution he was chairman
of the Petrograd Soviet. Following the Bolshevik seizure
of power he became first Commissar for Foreign Affairs
and was responsible for negotiating the Treaty of Brest-
Litovsk with Germany, ending Russia's participation in the
First World War. During the Russian Civil War he was
War Commissar and largely responsible for ensuring the
success of the Red Army against the Whites. A brilliant
orator and fluent polemicist and writer, Trotsky was
a charismatic figure who seemed the epitome of the
romantic revolutionary. He saw himself as Lenin's heir, but
was outmanoeuvred by Stalin. In 1927 he was expelled
from the Communist Party, and in 1929 he was expelled
from the Soviet Union. In exile, first in Turkey and then
in France and Mexico, he continued to oppose Stalinist
totalitarianism and founded the Fourth International.
Trotsky was assassinated by the Stalinist agent Ramon
Mercader, who stabbed him with an ice pick on 20 August
1940. He is shown here on his deathbed

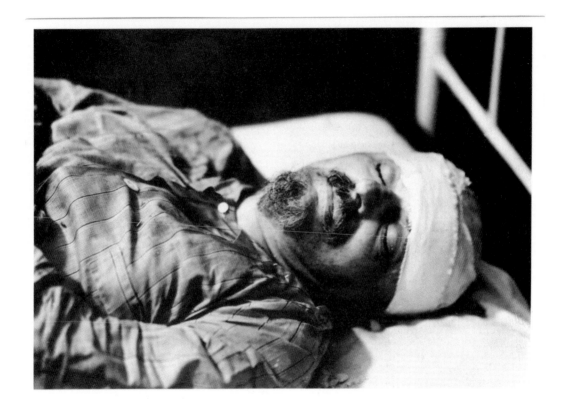

Tomáš Garrigue Masaryk (1850–1937)

A Czech philosopher and statesman, Masaryk was the founder and first president of an independent Czechoslavakia. The son of a coachman, he became an academic and was appointed Professor of Philosophy at Prague University in 1882. An advocate of greater cooperation between the Slavic nations, he was a member of the Austrian parliament from 1891 to 1893 as a member of the Young Czech Party, and again from 1907 to 1914 as a member of the Realist Party. At the beginning of the First World War he fled abroad to avoid arrest as a traitor, and in 1915 he became one of the first members of staff of the newly founded School of Slavonic and East European Studies in London. He spent much of the war in England, France, and the United States campaigning for Czechoslovak independence from the Austro-Hungarian Empire, and in 1917 he travelled to Russia to organize the Czech Legion to fight for the Allies on the Eastern Front. As the Austrian Empire collapsed in the closing weeks of the war, Masaryk proclaimed the independence of Czechoslovakia on the steps of Independence Hall, Philadelphia. Elected first President of Czechoslovakia in 1920, he was subsequently twice re-elected and only resigned in 1935 because of ill-health. Masaryk's reputation as the father of his people and a democratic philosopher-king remains very high.

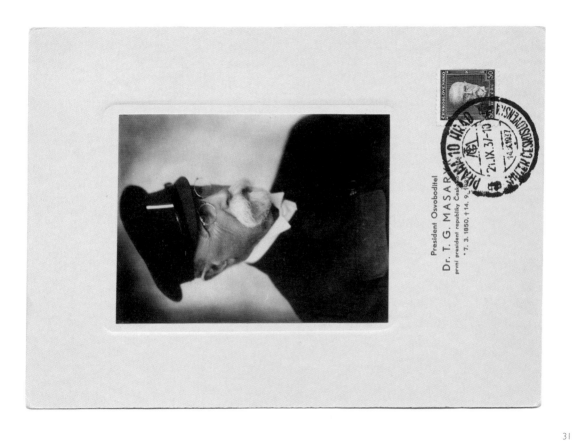

Miklós Horthy (1868–1957)

Regent of Hungary from 1920 to 1944, Admiral Horthy sometimes aroused derision through being regent of a kingdom which had no king, and admiral in a country which had neither navy nor coastline. Horthy's quarter century of rule in Hungary continues to arouse controversy, but is seen by some as an oasis of calm and stability in an otherwise turbulent century in Hungarian history. Born into a Protestant noble family, Horthy became a career officer in the Austro-Hungarian navy, eventually becoming its last Commander-in-Chief in the closing months of the First World War. Following the collapse of the Dual Monarchy, a Soviet government under Béla Kun was formed in Hungary in 1919. Anti-Communist elements coalesced around Horthy, who formed a National Army, and following the collapse of the Commune, occupied Budapest. He was then offered the regency on his own terms, and it has been argued that he ruled somewhat like an over-powerful constitutional monarch throughout the inter-war period. Opposed to political or social reform, his regime can be characterized as 'conservative-authoritarian'. Two policies dominated his thinking: anti-communism, which also embraced anti-Semitism, and revanchism, which reflected the desire to regain the territories Hungary had lost after the First World War through the Treaty of Trianon. Both policies led Horthy into what has been called a 'Faustian bargain' with Hitler. At first the policy was successful as Hungary regained parts of Slovakia, Ruthenia and Transylvania, but in 1941 Hungary was persuaded to take part in the German invasion of the USSR Faced with defeat, Horthy attempted to change sides in 1944 but was forestalled by the Germans, who forced him to resign and then deported him to Germany. Freed, and then arrested by the Americans, he escaped being tried as a war criminal at the insistence of Stalin, and lived the remainder of his life in exile in Portugal.

HORTHY MIKLÓS

MAGYARORSZÁG KORMÁNYZÓJA

Mustafa Kemal Atatürk (1881–1938)

An army officer who became a revolutionary statesman and the founder of modern Turkey, Kemal Atatürk served as president of his country from 1923 until his death in 1938. He was born in Thessaloniki in 1881 and joined the army in 1905. He soon demonstrated his commitment to reform and the modernization of Turkey when he played a role in the revolt of the Young Turks who overthrew the rule of the Sultan in 1908. After serving in Libya, Kemal made his name as a military commander at Gallipoli in the First World War. He subsequently fought in Anatolia against the Russians and in Palestine against British and Arab forces. Following the defeat of the Ottoman Empire in 1918, he led the Turkish national movement and established a provisional government in Ankara.

The victorious Allied powers had planned to partition Turkey, but Kemal was able to repel the Greek invasion of Anatolia, and, by the Treaty of Lausanne in 1923, to achieve international recognition of an independent Turkish republic. Elected president the same year, Kemal instituted a programme of reform and modernization. He rejected both communism and fascism, but instead aimed to turn Turkey into a Westernized, secular state. Western legal codes, the Western calendar, Western alphabet and Western dress were all introduced, the educational system was reformed and modernized, the status of women was improved, and a five-year plan of industrialization undertaken. The majority of Kemal's reforms have stood the test of time, and the guiding principles of Kemalism remain a significant feature of Turkey's political culture today.

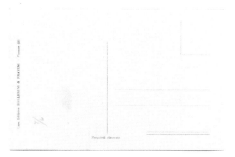

Benito Mussolini (1883–1945)

Known as 'Il Duce', Mussolini was the Fascist ruler of Italy from 1922 to 1943. Prior to the First World War he was a journalist in the socialist press, but his support for the war led to his breaking with the socialists. He served in the Italian army during the war, and after the war ended, founded the Fascist Party in 1919. Italy was then suffering from a period of political instability, and in 1922 Mussolini presented himself as the only person capable of restoring order. Following his carefully stage-managed 'March on Rome', Mussolini was appointed Prime Minister by the king. He set about replacing Italy's democratic institutions with a totalitarian state, and in 1925 proclaimed himself 'Il Duce', or leader. He instituted a programme of public works at home and became famous for 'making the trains run on time'. Abroad, he had ambitions to create a new 'Roman Empire' and to turn the Mediterranean into 'an Italian lake'. In 1923 he invaded and occupied Corfu and shortly afterwards set up a puppet regime in Albania. In 1935 he invaded Ethiopia, and in 1939 Albania was formally annexed to Italy and King Zog forced to flee. Mussolini joined the 'Pact of Steel' with Hitler, declaring war on Britain and France when he thought Hitler had already won the war. Swiftly disillusioned, Mussolini saw his forces suffer defeat by the British navy in the Mediterranean and by the British army in East and North Africa. His invasion of Greece proved no more successful, and German troops had to be sent to help him shore up all these fronts. In 1943 the Allies invaded Italy and Mussolini was dismissed by the king following a successful coup by some of his former Fascist colleagues. Italy changed sides, but Mussolini was rescued by German paratroopers and installed as titular ruler of a pocket state in the north of Italy. Captured by partisans, he was executed on 28 April 1945.

S. E. BENITO MUSSOLINI

1177

Foto Pettini

37

POST CARD

ADDRESS

WHY I SUPPORT FRANCO. "It is a struggle of civilisation against barbarism." The late Miguel de Unamuno, one of the world's greatest Liberals and intellectual leaders, Rector of Salamanca University.

Francisco Franco (1892–1975)

Caudillo of Spain from the end of the Civil War to his death, Franco was the last of the fascist leaders of the 1930s to remain in power. Franco made his name as a ruthless commander of the Spanish Foreign Legion in North Africa in the 1920s. He displayed the same characteristics when putting down a strike of coalminers in the Asturias. Distrusted by the Republican government that came to power in 1931, Franco was sidelined by being made Governor of the Canary Islands in 1936. However, this proved a mistake, as he then led the Army of Africa across the straits to the Spanish mainland to support a military revolt against the government. This developed into the Spanish Civil War, in which, aided by the fascist governments of Italy and Germany, Franco's nationalist forces emerged victorious. He founded the Falange Party and established a classic authoritarian government of the right. In 1947 he was declared Head of State for life. After the fall of France in 1940 it seemed possible that Spain would enter the war on the side of the Axis, and Hitler met Franco at Hendaye to try and persuade him to do so. However, Franco's extensive demands – he wanted Gibraltar and most of French North Africa for Spain whilst offering little in return – led to an unsatisfactory conclusion to the talks, Hitler later claiming that he would rather have his teeth drawn than go through such an experience again. Undoubtedly it was Franco's decision not to enter the Second World War that ensured his survival. Some believe this reflects not so much Franco's political skill, but rather Spain's poverty and inability to fight a war, allied to a fear that the British would blockade the country and seize the Canary Islands immediately hostilities broke out. Franco's survival in the years following the war was largely due to his anti-communist stance, which appealed to the Americans, who were granted military bases in Spain after 1953. Franco's authoritarian regime was swiftly dismantled after his death, and within seven years Spain was a democratic constitutional monarchy and a member of the European Community.

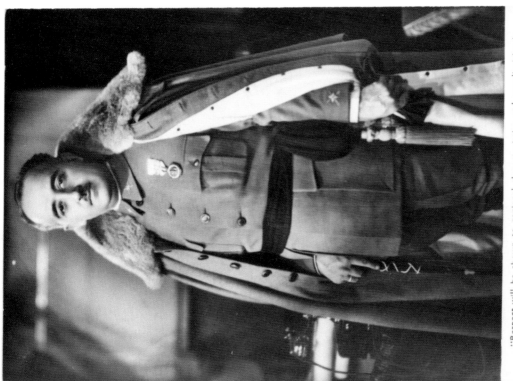

"Respect will be shown to regional characteristics and peculiarities in harmony with the ancient national traditions in the best days of our national splendour, but without allowing any harm to be done to the national unity''.—General Franco

39

Adolf Hitler (1889–1945)

Founder of the Nazi Party, Reich Chancellor and then Führer of Germany from 1933 until his suicide in the ruins of Berlin in 1945, Hitler rose to power following imprisonment (during which he dictated his political ideas in *Mein Kampf*) after a failed coup in Munich. Riding on a wave of European fascism in the 1920s and early 1930s he proved a highly effective communicator and propagandist, promoting nationalism and promising to cure Germany's post-war malaise. At a time of social, political, and economic upheaval, he blamed many of Germany's problems on Jews and Bolsheviks.

Once elected, he ruthlessly eliminated all opposition, established a totalitarian and fascist dictatorship, instituted anti-Jewish laws, and rearmed Germany.

Germany's invasion of Poland in September 1939, which marked the start of the Second World War, was followed by military success throughout Europe. Having lost the Battle of Britain in 1941, Hitler ordered the invasion of the Soviet Union and declared war on the USA. Responsible for the death of six million Jews and two million gypsies, his policies resulted ultimately in the deaths of an estimated forty-six million people worldwide and the destruction of much of Europe's civilization. This, together with his ideas of a 'National Socialist race', have made him for many the icon of evil.

Der FÜHRER am Hintersee bei Berchtesgaden

41

Winston Churchill (1874–1965)

In the years before his death, Winston Churchill was regularly referred to as 'the greatest living Englishman' and more recently he was voted the winner in a BBC poll to find the 'Greatest Briton'. Despite his anti-communist stance, which led him to promote intervention in Russia after the First World War, Stalin later characterized him as a 'man who is born once in a hundred years'. Churchill's political career was remarkable for its longevity – he first entered the Cabinet in 1908 and finally resigned as Prime Minister in 1955 – but also for its unevenness.

He crossed the floor of the House of Commons from the Conservatives to the Liberals and back again, and spent the 1930s out of office in what he termed 'the wilderness years'. Nor was he regarded as successful in all the Cabinet posts he held, being widely blamed for the Gallipoli campaign in the First World War, and accused of being an unsuccessful Chancellor of the Exchequer in the 1920s. Yet on the central question of his time, recognizing and then resisting the Nazi threat, he was clear sighted, and he owes his reputation above all for rallying the British people to continue the fight in the dark days of 1940, when Britain stood alone, and then mobilizing and inspiring the coalition that defeated the Axis powers. Churchill is widely regarded as Britain's greatest war leader, rivalling both elder and younger Pitts and Lloyd George. A great orator and popularizer of the phrase 'Iron Curtain', he was also a writer of note (who won the Nobel Prize for Literature) and a painter of more than average talent. As his successor, Clement Attlee, wrote, he was 'rather like a layer cake', part seventeenth-century, part eighteenth, part nineteenth, a large slice of the twentieth, and 'another, curious layer which may possibly have been the twenty-first'.

THE RT. HON. WINSTON L. S. CHURCHILL, OM CH

43

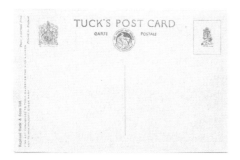

Franklin Delano Roosevelt (1882–1945)

Thirty-second President of the United States and the only man to be elected to that office four times, many regard FDR – as he was known – as the greatest of all American presidents. Born in upstate New York, and brought up in an atmosphere of privilege, he was first elected for the Democrats to the New York Senate in 1910 and later served as Assistant Secretary of the Navy under Wilson. He ran for Vice-President in 1920 but was defeated. He contracted polio, but continued to be active in politics and was elected Governor of New York in 1928. He was first elected President of the USA in 1932 at the height of the Great Depression, and immediately declared his intent to be an interventionist president in his inaugural address, in the course of which he declared: 'We have nothing to fear but fear itself.' His New Deal programme sought to pull America out of the Depression through public works, measures to stimulate the economy, reform of the banking sector and measures to provide for unemployment relief. In foreign affairs FDR aimed to maintain America's traditional neutrality, but after the fall of France in 1940 he sent aid to Britain under the Lend-Lease programme. After Japan attacked Pearl Harbor in December 1941 – 'a day that will live in infamy' in the President's words – he mobilized all of America's human and material resources to ensure total victory over both Japan and Germany. Rather like Churchill, he became to many a symbol of the free world, and, with Churchill and Stalin, he was one of the 'big three' who directed the Allied war effort. He has been accused of giving in too easily to Stalin's desires at the Allied conference at Yalta, but America nevertheless emerged from the Second World War as one of the world's only two superpowers. By then Roosevelt was dead, dying of a cerebral haemorrhage just a few weeks before victory in Europe.

President Roosevelt als grootvader

Emperor Haile Selassie (1892–1975)

Known as the 'Lion of Judah', Haile Selassie claimed to be a direct descendant of the Queen of Sheba and King Solomon, and to some in the Rastafari movement he continues to be regarded as a religious symbol of God incarnate. He was born into the Ethiopian royal family, but at the time of his birth it was by no means certain that he would become Emperor. However, following a coup in 1916, in which Iyasu V was replaced by the Empress Zweditu, Haile Selassie became regent and de facto ruler of Ethiopia, and in 1930, when Zweditu died in somewhat mysterious circumstances, he became Emperor in his own name. He adopted a policy of modernization, hoping that this would protect Ethiopia from economic imperialism, and in 1931 he introduced the first written constitution to the country. However, none of these measures was sufficient to prevent the Italian invasion of Ethiopia in 1935, and Haile Selassie was forced into exile. He appeared before the League of Nations to plead his case, and both his speech and his own calm dignity immediately made him an icon for anti-fascists throughout the world. In 1936 he moved to England, only returning to Ethiopia after the defeat of the Italians in the Second World War. In the ensuing decades Ethiopia appeared an island of stability in Africa. Haile Selassie was a staunch ally of the West, whilst simultaneously supporting decolonization in Africa and becoming a founder member of the Organization of African Unity which was based in Addis Ababa. Below the surface, however, there was considerable unrest. The Emperor was overthrown by a military coup in 1974 and spent his last months imprisoned in one of his palaces.

Emperor Hirohito (1901–89)

Japanese Emperor from 1926 until his death in 1989, Hirohito's reign encompassed the rise of militarism in Japan itself, Japan's invasion of Manchuria and then of the rest of China in the 1930s, an initial period of success in the Second World War, in which Japanese forces overran the European empires in South-East Asia, followed by a crushing defeat at the hands of the United States, a military occupation by the Americans, and the gradual rise of a newly democratic Japan to become the economic powerhouse of Asia. How much influence the Emperor himself had on any of these events has remained a matter of controversy, with some arguing that he was little more than a figurehead, whilst other scholars have pointed to documents that show him intervening decisively in the political process in the 1930s and 1940s. Some think he was neither bellicose nor a pacifist, but essentially an opportunist. What is beyond dispute, however, is that it was his decisive intervention after the dropping of the atomic bomb that led to Japan's unconditional surrender. Broadcasting for the first time, he told his people that 'the war situation has developed not necessarily to Japan's advantage', and that they should 'endure the unendurable' by surrendering. It was the first time the vast majority of Japanese had heard their Emperor speak and the broadcast had a profound and lasting impact. It might have been thought that the victorious Allies would insist on deposing the Emperor, but General MacArthur, the American viceroy, saw him as a symbol of continuity and cohesion. He was, however, stripped of all political power, and spent the rest of his reign as the symbolic head of state only. The Emperor was also a marine biologist of some distinction, who published articles under his own name in various scholarly journals. This postcard, in German, probably dates from the late 1930s.

Kaiser HIROHITO
Tenno von Japan

Chiang Kai-shek (1887–1975)

Generalissimo of the nationalist government of China from 1928 onwards, Chiang Kai-shek was seen as a key ally by the West during the Second World War. After his defeat by Mao Zedong and the subsequent establishment of the People's Republic of China, he was left in control only of the island of Taiwan.

A supporter of Sun Yat Sen's nationalist Kuomintang party, Chiang became one of the leaders of the KMT after Sun's death in 1925. This was at a time of political disintegration and 'warlordism' in China, and Chiang led the army that aimed to unify the country. After breaking with the Communists, Chiang established a nationalist government in Nanjing. From 1928 to 1937 Chiang followed a policy of economic and social reform, and in 1934 he established the New Life Movement, which, being based on traditional Confuciansm, was intended to act as an antidote to Communism. After the Japanese invasion in 1937 Chiang was forced to move his government to Chonqing. There he received considerable aid from the British and Americans in his fight against the Japanese, although some observers believed that he devoted more energy to fighting internal enemies, such as the Communists, than he did to fighting the invader. As soon as the Second World War was over a civil war broke out in China between the Nationalists and the Communists. In this Chiang was defeated, and in 1949 he fled to Taiwan, where he established a one-party government, which, dominated by Chinese exiles from the mainland, claimed sovereignty over all of China. During the Cold War Chiang was sustained in this by the USA, until Nixon's rapprochement with the People's Republic brought about a rapid change in policy.

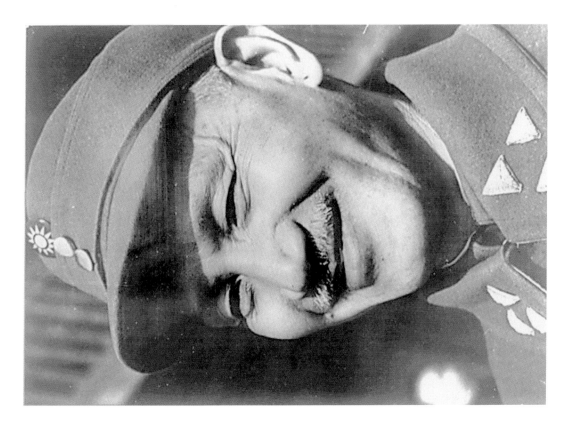

Jawaharlal Nehru (1889–1964) and Mohandas K. Gandhi (1869–1948)

Gandhi and Nehru, although very different in personality, formed an effective partnership in leading India to independence in 1947. Thereafter, Nehru served as Prime Minister of India until his death in 1964.

Nehru (left) was an intellectual and a patrician who was deeply committed to democracy and to good governance, as well as to improving the lot of India's poor and disadvantaged. His vision was for a modernized, secular India, which could lead the way internationally in establishing a more peaceful post-colonial world.

Economically, he promoted socialist policies and adopted the first of India's five-year plans. Internationally, he became a leading member of the Non-Aligned Movement. Some see the Chinese invasion of India's northern border regions in 1962 as a severe blow to his prestige which undermined his authority at home in his last years.

To most Indians, Gandhi (right) came to personify the Freedom Struggle. A man of both vision and action, his thought was complex, and in advocating *swaraj* (self-rule) for India he had in mind not just political freedom but a total moral and social transformation. He also believed in non-violent resistance, or *satyagraha*, and it was the implementation of this policy against the British Raj that gave his independence campaign its extraordinary moral force. Fully aware of the power of symbols, his Salt March to the sea in 1930 is regarded as a brilliantly staged piece of political protest, which impressed friends and foes alike. Opposed to Partition, Gandhi was deeply shocked by the violence that broke out at the time of Independence, and his hunger strike was widely credited with preventing the violence spreading to Calcutta. Assassinated by a Hindu fanatic in 1948, he came to be seen as both a martyr and a saint, even though few Indians then or since have chosen to follow his path of self-imposed poverty and asceticism. 'A man for all times and all place', Gandhi's moral stature remains high.

Eva Perón (1919–52)

Maria Eva Duarte de Perón, more commonly called Evita, was the second wife of Juan Perón and the First Lady of Argentina from 1946 until her death. A popular radio actress, who amongst other roles played Elizabeth I, she married Perón in 1945. She became a powerful and glamorous figure in the Perónist trade unions, speaking up for the poor and the disadvantaged, and founded and ran her own political party, the Female Perónist Party. It was partly owing to her advocacy that women were given the vote in Argentina, and she mobilized their support for Perón in the 1952 elections, the first in which they could vote. Through her charity, the Eva Perón Foundation, Evita provided considerable support for Argentina's poor and came to be regarded as almost a saint by many of them. Evita became the object of a personality cult, which she herself encouraged, for example through her 'Rainbow Tour' of Europe in 1947. Prevented by the military from standing as Vice-President in the 1952 elections, Evita was shortly afterwards proclaimed the 'Spiritual Leader of the Nation' but died only a month later of cancer. The combination of her femininity, perceived spirituality, and revolutionary views has ensured that Evita remains a powerful icon in Argentina today, and the musical *Evita* by Andrew Lloyd Webber has contributed to the perpetuation of the myth of the woman whom Tomás Martinez has dubbed 'The Cinderella of the Tango'.

Charles de Gaulle (1890–1970)

Like Louis XIV before him, who declared 'L'État, c'est moi', de Gaulle dominated French politics. The defining moment of de Gaulle's career came in 1940, when, on the fall of France he fled to England and broadcast to his countrymen urging them to continue the fight. Throughout the war he remained leader of the Free French, and maintained 'une certaine idée de la France', despite feeling snubbed by his 'Anglo-Saxon' allies. In 1944 de Gaulle entered Paris with his troops ahead of the British and the Americans, thereby establishing the myth that the French had liberated themselves.

As President of the Provisional Government he aimed to restore France's position as a great power, but in 1946 he resigned as he felt the new Constitution of the Fourth Republic gave insufficient powers to the presidency. Political instability and military defeats in French Indo-China and Algeria led to the collapse of the Fourth Republic, and de Gaulle returned to reclaim power and create the Fifth Republic, whose Constitution was much more to his liking. De Gaulle oversaw a rapprochement between France and Germany and was a strong supporter of a French-led Europe with a strong global presence. He envisaged a Europe 'from the Atlantic to the Urals', but twice vetoed Britain's application to join the EEC. During 'les événements' of May 1968, de Gaulle at one point fled to Germany and considered using the army to put down the protests, but returned to negotiate with the protesters, declaring 'la réforme oui, la chienlit non', a phrase which has since passed into legend. He resigned the Presidency the following year.

Our great leader Chairman Mao
Notre grand dirigeant, le président Mao
Nuestro gran líder el Presidente Mao

Foreign Languages Press Peking
Editions en Langues Étrangères Pékin

Mao Zedong (1893–1976)

'The Great Helmsman', a leader of the Chinese Communist Party from the 1920s, the founder of the People's Republic of China in 1949 and effective ruler of China from then until his death in 1976, Mao was also a dictator who encouraged a personality cult. After the Kuomintang broke with the Communists, Mao successfully led his army on the Long March to Yan'an. Mao overturned Lenin's doctrine by basing his revolutionary campaign on the rural rather than the urban proletariat, a strategy that ultimately led to the Communists emerging victorious in the Chinese civil war. The Great Leap Forward (1957–9), which took the ideas of collectivization and forced industrialization to new levels, has been directly linked to what became the greatest man-made famine in human history, in which around twenty million people died. Faced with opposition from within the Communist Party, Mao in 1966 unleashed the Cultural Revolution in which he encouraged the Red Guards to overthrow existing authority (other than his own). During this period the cult of Mao's personality reached new heights, with the *Little Red Book* of his sayings being regarded as the only authoritative text. Although the Cultural Revolution officially ended in 1968, the leftists around Mao remained in control of China until his death. Mao broke away from a Communist model dominated by the Soviet Union and by the 1970s sought a measure of rapprochement with the USA. Subsequent Chinese governments, whilst never officially repudiating Mao, have reversed almost all his economic policies. Nevertheless, Maoism remains a potent revolutionary doctrine, especially in the poorer countries of the developing world.

我們的伟大领袖毛主席

Ho Chi Minh (1890–1969)

Ho Chi Minh was a Vietnamese nationalist and revolutionary who became the symbol of his country's resistance to French, Japanese, and American imperialism. Born in what was then French Indo-China, he later moved to Europe, working in England for a time as a waiter. In 1920 he became a founder member of the French Communist Party and later moved to the Soviet Union and then China. During the Second World War he led the Viet Minh resistance movement against both the Vichy French and the Japanese occupation of Vietnam, and in 1945 he declared the independence of the Democratic Republic of Vietnam. When the great powers reinstated the French as rulers of Vietnam, he continued the fight and secured a decisive victory over the French at Dien Bien Phu in 1954. Vietnam was then partitioned, with Ho Chi Minh becoming President of North Vietnam. However, he continued to press for the unification of the country and in 1960 formed the National Front for the Liberation of South Vietnam. The United States entered the war to shore up the South Vietnamese regime, and Ho became an icon to many anti-Vietnam War protesters worldwide. Ho died in 1969, but six years later the war ended in victory for North Vietnam and the unification of the country to which Ho had devoted his life.

Josip Broz Tito (1892–1980)

The last of the statesmen who came to power at the end of the Second World War to remain in office, Tito is regarded by some historians as the only European communist leader outside Russia to display a certain level of both independence and statesmanship. Born in what is now Croatia, he worked as a mechanic before being conscripted into the Austro-Hungarian army during the First World War. Captured by the Russians, he became a communist and took part in the Russian Revolution in 1917. A member of the Comintern, Tito fought in the Spanish Civil War, before returning to Yugoslavia and becoming a leader of the partisans during the Second World War. The partisans were able to liberate Yugoslavia largely free of Soviet assistance, and it was this which enabled Tito subsequently to break with Stalin and assert Yugoslavia's autonomy in 1948. Thereafter he followed a policy of 'positive neutrality' abroad, whilst his internal policy of 'democratic socialism' allowed a greater degree of individual liberty and enterprise than elsewhere in the Communist bloc. Yugoslavia remained unified after his death until the end of the Cold War, when a vicious inter-ethnic conflict broke out, leading to new political entities in the region.

Kwame Nkrumah (1909–72) with Jawaharlal Nehru

As leader of Ghana, the first black African colony to gain its independence, Kwame Nkrumah (right) was an inspirational figure to those fighting colonialism throughout the world and especially in Africa. Educated partly in the United States and Britain, he helped to organize the Pan-African Congress in 1945. Returning to Ghana in 1947, two years later he founded the Convention People's Party, which campaigned for independence from Great Britian. As a result of the CPP's 'positive action' campaign, Nkrumah was imprisoned in 1950, but the CPP won the election in 1951 and Nkrumah was released from jail to become Prime Minister. In 1957 Ghana became independent from the British Empire with Nkrumah as its first President. He instituted a comprehensive programme of social and economic development. A strong supporter of Pan-Africanism, he believed that all of black Africa needed to be united politically and he was one of the founders of the Organization of African Unity. He instituted a one-party state in 1964 and declared himself President for life. This, allied to a declining economy, led to increasing opposition to his rule, and in 1966, whilst out of the country, he was overthrown by a military coup, which received support from Western countries. He spent the rest of his life in exile, dying in Bucharest, Romania.

Gamal Abdel Nasser (1918–70)

One of the leaders of the 1952 Egyptian Revolution and the country's second President, serving from 1954 until his death in 1970, Nasser was a charismatic figure who became a hero to Arab nationalists throughout the Middle East. The son of a postal worker, Nasser joined the Egyptian army in 1938 and fought in the first Arab–Israeli war in 1948, a war that led to Israel's independence. Along with a group of other army officers he founded the Free Officers Movement that overthrew King Farouk in 1952. Two years later he deposed the first President of Egypt, General Naguib in a military coup to become President himself. Nasser was a supporter of Arab nationalism throughout the region and supported anti-colonial and Arab national movements in the Yemen, Libya, Iraq, and Algeria. He also believed in Pan-Arabism, which led to the short-lived political union of Egypt and Syria as the United Arab Republic in 1958, and was a founding member of the Non-Aligned Movement. At heart, however, Nasser was an Egyptian nationalist and his action in nationalizing the Suez Canal, and in seeing off the British, French, and Israeli invasion of Suez in 1956 brought his popularity within Egypt and the Arab world to new heights. Domestically, his government tried to improve the lot of the rural poor and a programme of land reform was instituted, and when the West refused to finance the building of the Aswan Dam he turned to the Soviet Union for help. However, the Arab defeat by Israel in the Six Day War of 1967 ended of his dream of Pan-Arabism. It is a mark of his popularity in Egypt that he survived this defeat and remained President until his death three years later.

Fidel Castro (1926–   )

Castro's image as the perpetual revolutionary, often dressed in battle fatigues, together with his defiance of the United States for half a century, has made him a hero to many in the developing world. Known even in his student days as a radical nationalist, deeply opposed to the overpowering influence of the USA in Cuba, in 1953 he led an uprising against the dictatorship of General Batista with an attack on the Moncada Barracks. This failed and after a period of imprisonment he went into exile in Mexico where he founded the 26th July Movement (named after the date of the attack). In 1956 he invaded Cuba with a small group of revolutionaries and led them in a guerrilla war against the Batista government. On 1 January 1959 Batista fled, and a week later Castro entered Havana in triumph. He ruled the country for the ensuing forty-nine years until ill-health forced his retirement from the presidency in 2008. To a great extent, Castro's defiance of the American embargo of Cuba, and his defeat of the failed American invasion at the Bay of Pigs in 1961 raised his standing. He also survived over six hundred assassination attempts, which included such devices as exploding cigars and a fungal-infected diving suit. To counter the American blockade Castro turned to the Soviet Union. Soviet attempts to install missiles on the island led to the Cuban Missile Crisis of 1962. In 1965 he turned Cuba into a one-party socialist state. During the Cold War, Cuban troops were often used as surrogates by the Soviet Union, as in the Angolan Civil War. Castro survived the collapse of the Soviet Union in 1991, and was able to hand over power peacefully to his brother, Raúl, in 2008.

Ernesto 'Che' Guevara (1928–67)

The epitome of the romantic revolutionary and guerrilla fighter, Che's image remains an icon for revolutionaries throughout the world. He was born in Rosario, Argentina, in 1928 and trained to become a medical doctor. Whilst still a medical student he travelled through much of Latin America and was appalled by the poverty he witnessed. He turned to Marxism and came to believe that the only solution to the region's problems was a total social and political revolution. He believed that capitalism was a 'contest among wolves' and that material incentives should be replaced by moral ones, creating 'a new man and a new woman' and a 'unity between the individual and the mass'. He moved to Guatemala to witness the social reforms of the Arbenz government, and when Arbenz was overthrown by a CIA-inspired coup, he was confirmed in his hostility to American imperialism in Latin America. Two years later he joined Fidel Castro in Mexico and was one of the group of revolutionaries who invaded Cuba in 1956 with the aim of overthrowing the Batista government, widely seen as a puppet of the United States. Guevara played a key role in the guerrilla war that led to the fall of Batista and the establishment of a revolutionary socialist government under Castro. He held a number of different government posts under Castro, including acting as the government prosecutor of 'revolutionary justice' against supporters of the previous regime, and wrote an influential manual on the theory and practice of guerrilla warfare. In 1965 he left Cuba to incite revolution elsewhere. Two years later he was captured in Bolivia with the help of the CIA and executed. His death in such circumstances only served to enhance his almost mythical status as the ultimate revolutionary hero.

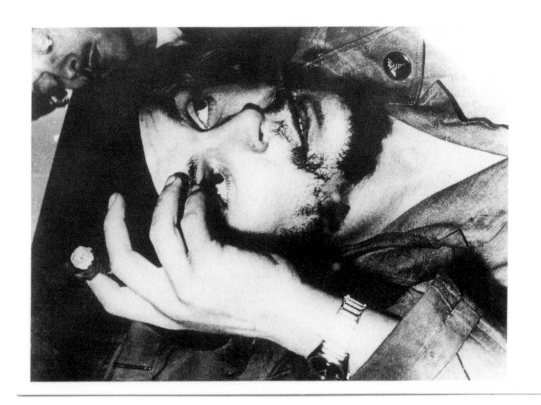

Nikita Khrushchev (1894–1971) with John F. Kennedy (1917–63)

Grandson of a serf, Nikita Khrushchev (left) joined the Bolsheviks shortly after the October Revolution and fought in the Red Army during the Civil War. After rising through the ranks of the Communist Party under Stalin, Khrushchev eventually emerged victorious from the power struggle that followed Stalin's death. He was ruler of the Soviet Union from 1955 to 1964, when he was ousted in a coup. Khrushchev's record is mixed. He denounced Stalin in his famous 'secret speech' and introduced a certain degree of liberalization into the Soviet system, but also suppressed the Hungarian Uprising of 1956. A tough negotiator, he may have agreed to remove the Soviet missiles from Cuba in 1962 after the dramatic missile crisis, but received in return a pledge from Kennedy that American missiles would be removed from northern Turkey. British Prime Minister Harold Macmillan characterized him as 'a very clever man, very well informed … impulsive; sensitive of his own dignity and insensitive to anyone else's feelings; quick in argument …; vulgar, and yet capable of a certain dignity when he is simple and forgets to "show off"; ruthless but sentimental'. He is remembered by some for his bombastic ebullience and for the incident on 11 October 1960 at the UN General Assembly when, inflamed by a remark by the Filipino delegate Lorenzo Sumulong which castigated the USSR for the extent of its influence in Eastern Europe, Khrushchev brandished his shoe in the air and allegedly banged it on the table.

John F. Kennedy, with Robert F. Kennedy (1925–68) and Edward Kennedy (1932–   )

The election of John F. Kennedy (far right) as America's thirty-fifth President in 1960 marked a clean break with the past. He was the eldest of these brothers of the wealthy, Roman Catholic Kennedy family. Young and glamorous, he seemed the polar opposite of his predecessor, Eisenhower. As Harold Macmillan later wrote, 'Kennedy meant youth, energy, idealism and a new hope for the world.' The achievements of his administration did not always match up to the image, but Kennedy showed courage in resolving the Cuban Missile Crisis in 1962, whilst the establishment of the Peace Corps remains one of his most enduring achievements. His assassination in Dallas in 1963 cut short a presidency that still promised much, and some say that everyone alive at the time can remember where they were when they heard the news.

Robert (Bobby) Kennedy (far left) was US Attorney-General in JFK's administration and served subsequently as Senator for New York. Bobby Kennedy was a supporter of the civil rights movement, and was on the liberal wing of the Democratic Party, opposing President Johnson's Vietnam policy. In 1968 he announced that he was running for President, but was assassinated the day after winning the crucial California primary.

Edward Kennedy (middle) has been Senator for Massachusetts and a leading liberal in the Democratic Party since being first elected in 1962. He has promoted many liberal causes, including same-sex marriages, greater levels of gun control in America and a range of environmental protection measures.

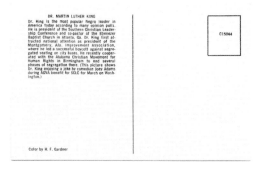

Martin Luther King (1929–68)

A Baptist minister, Martin Luther King was one of the main leaders of the American civil rights movement. In 1955–6 he led the black boycott of racially segregated buses in Montgomery, Alabama, and gained a major victory when the buses were desegregated in 1956. In 1957 he was elected leader of the Southern Christian Leadership Conference, which provided a new focus for the civil rights movement. It has been estimated that over the next eleven years King travelled over six million miles and addressed around 2,500 meetings in support of civil rights campaigns across America. He followed Gandhi in advocating non-violent direct action, and he was arrested many times during the 1950s and 1960s. The climax of his campaign was the march on Washington, DC in 1963, during which he made his famous 'I have a dream' speech. Although he was never a member of Congress, the Civil Rights Act of 1964 and the Voting Rights Act of 1965, which saw many of his goals realized, are seen to a large extent as his legacy. On 4 April 1968 King was shot dead by an assassin in Memphis, Tennessee. King was awarded the Nobel Peace Prize in 1964, and in 1983 the third Monday of January (close to King's birthday on the 15th) was declared a US public holiday. Although some US states were at first reluctant to observe the holiday, in 2000, for the first time, it was observed across the country.

Dr. King

77

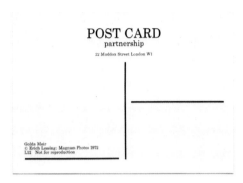

POST CARD
partnership
22 Maddox Street London W1

Golda Meir
© Erich Lessing: Magnum Photos 1972
L12 Not for reproduction

Golda Meir (1898–1978)

A founder of the State of Israel, and the country's fourth Prime Minister, serving from 1969 to 1974, Mrs Meir was a formidable politician. Long before Margaret Thatcher came on the scene, she was known as the 'Iron Lady', and David Ben-Gurion said that she was 'the only man in the government'. She was born Golda Mabovitch in Kiev, but, to escape from anti-Jewish pogroms, her family emigrated to the United States in 1906 and she spent her formative years in Milwaukee, Wisconsin. Whilst a student she became a Socialist Zionist. She married Morris Meyerson in 1917 and the couple moved to Palestine in 1921, where they found work on a kibbutz. Mrs Meir (who changed her name at David Ben-Gurion's urging) became acting head of the Political Department of the Jewish Agency in 1946, and she was one of the twenty-four signatories of the Israeli Declaration of Independence in 1948. Sent to raise money for the new state in the United States, she later became Israel's first ambassador to the USSR She was elected to the Knesset in 1949 and remained a member until her resignation in 1974. A member of the Israeli Labour Party, she was Minister of Labour from 1949 to 1956 and Foreign Minister from 1956 to 1966. Despite having retired on health grounds, she was recalled to become Prime Minister in 1969. Although she was accused of contributing to Israel's unpreparedness at the start of the Yom Kippur War in 1973, she won the subsequent general election, but resigned soon afterwards.

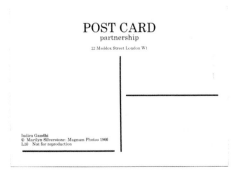

POST CARD
partnership
22 Maddox Street London W1

Indira Gandhi
© Marilyn Silverstone: Magnum Photos 1966
L10   Not for reproduction

Indira Gandhi (1917–84)

The daughter of Jawaharlal Nehru, Mrs Gandhi served four terms as Prime Minister of India. After being educated in Switzerland and at Somerville College, Oxford, she returned to India in 1941 and married the journalist Feroze Gandhi a year later. Although not herself a leading member of the movement for Indian independence, through her father she knew most of the leaders of the Indian National Congress. She was first elected to parliament in 1964, and was appointed Minister of Information and Broadcasting in Lal Bahadur Shastri's government. When Shastri unexpectedly died in 1966, she became Prime Minister as a compromise candidate. Not expected to remain in the post for long, she showed considerable political skill in outmanoeuvring her opponents and consolidating her position. A populist, she adopted left-wing economic policies, and achieved great popularity after India's defeat of Pakistan in the 1971 war to liberate Bangladesh. However, in June 1975 the High Court found her guilty of political corruption and she was called on to resign. Her response was to proclaim a State of Emergency and rule unconstitutionally. This period was marked by increasing authoritarianism, exemplified by forced sterilization of the poor in an effort to solve India's population problem, although also by the policies of slum clearance in the cities. Believing that she had destroyed any opposition, Mrs Gandhi called a general election in 1977 and was defeated. She returned to power at the following election in 1980. Her last term in office was dominated by the rise of the Sikh secessionist movement in the Punjab. In June 1984 she sent in the army to attack the militant Sikhs who had occupied the Golden Temple in Amritsar. Militarily successful, this action led directly to her assassination by two Sikh members of her bodyguard the following November.

Muhammad Anwar al–Sadat (1918–81), and Muhammad Hosni Mubarak (1928–   )

Sadat (right) was the third President of Egypt, serving from 1970 until his assassination in 1981, moments after this photograph was taken. He was succeeded by his Vice-President, Hosni Mubarak (left), whose hand was injured in the attack.

Sadat was an army officer who was a member of the Free Officers Movement which overthrew the Egyptian monarchy in the revolution of 1952. He was a close ally of President Nasser whom he succeeded in 1970, after serving as Vice-President from 1964 to 1966 and again from 1969. At the time he was virtually unknown, but he swiftly established a firm hold over the country. His leadership in the 1973 Yom Kippur War against Israel, during which the Egyptian army gained an initial success in over-running much of the Sinai Peninsula, increased

his popularity, but the deteriorating economic situation in Egypt made him determined to establish peace with Israel. The negotiations were long and difficult, but in 1979 the Egypt–Israel Peace treaty was signed in Washington, DC, following the Camp David Accords, in which US President Jimmy Carter played a major role as mediator. Sadat and the Israeli Prime Minister Menachem Begin were awarded the Nobel Peace Prize, but Egypt was expelled from the Arab League, and the Egyptian economy did not benefit from the 'peace dividend' to the extent that Sadat expected. Increasingly unpopular at home, Sadat was assassinated during the annual 6th October victory parade in Cairo. Mubarak remains President of Egypt, having been re-elected on four successive occasions.

Yasser Arafat (1929–2004)

Chairman of the Palestine Liberation Organization, President of the Palestine National Authority and founder of Fatah, his political party, Arafat was effectively leader of the Palestinian people for forty years. Born Mohammed Abdel-Raouf Arafat al-Qudwa al-Husseini in Cairo and the son of a Palestinian textile merchant, at the age of seventeen he became engaged in supplying arms to Palestine. He fought in the Arab–Israeli War of 1948 and ten years later founded Fatah, which advocated armed struggle against Israel. Four years after it was founded in 1964, Arafat became Chairman of the Palestine Liberation Organization. In exile in Jordan, he made the PLO into a state within a state, until King Hussein, alarmed by the PLO's violent methods, expelled it. Arafat then attempted to create a similar organization in Lebanon but was forced to leave by an Israeli military invasion. He moved to Tunis, but this period saw the PLO at a low ebb, until the rise of the Intifada in Palestine itself. In 1988 Arafat changed policy and declared that the PLO had renounced violence and supported 'the right of all parties concerned in the Middle East conflict to live in peace and security'. He took part in a series of negotiations with Israel, which led to the Oslo Accord in 1993. For this agreement Arafat received the Nobel Peace Prize in 1994, and in 1996 he was elected first President of the newly formed Palestine National Authority. However, the peace process stalled, and Arafat found his position challenged by the more militant Hamas grouping. He spent the last two years of his life effectively confined to his compound in Ramallah by the Israeli army. Regarded as a hero by most Palestinians, he was also considered a terrorist by most Israelis, and was unable to achieve a lasting peace between the two.

Steve Biko   2.5.11. '89

Printed by Trojan Press 01-249 5771

Collets International, 129-131 Charing Cross Road, London WC2H OEQ

Steve Biko (1946–77)

An anti-Apartheid activist and founder of the Black Consciousness Movement whose brutal death at the hands of the South African police in 1977 shocked many people around the world, Biko was born in 1946 at King William's Town in the Eastern Cape. When a medical student, he founded the South African Students' Organization to campaign on behalf of black students, who felt unrepresented by the official National Union of South African Students. In 1972 he founded the Black Peoples Convention, and later coined the slogan 'Black is beautiful'. Between 1975 and 1977 he was arrested and interrogated four times for opposing the National Party government, but, despite the restrictions placed on his movements,

his Black Consciousness Movement played a leading role in the Soweto Uprising of 1976. Detained by police in Port Elizabeth in August 1977, Biko was found naked in his cell suffering from major head injuries. Transferred to Pretoria, he died of brain damage on 12 September. The South African authorities first claimed he died of a hunger strike, and then ensured that none of the police officers responsible for his murder were charged. Biko became a symbol of black resistance and an icon of the anti-Apartheid struggle. After the fall of Apartheid, the Truth and Reconciliation Commission reported that his death was 'a result of injuries sustained during his detention', and that five officers had applied for amnesty.

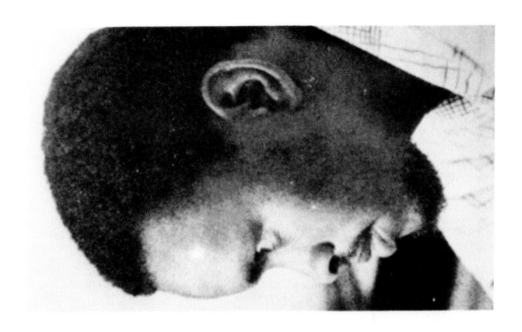

----------IMAM KHOMEINI----------

1) THE UNCOMPROMISING STRUGGLE OF OUR NATION AGAINST ALL OPPRESSORS WILL CONTINUE TILL THE END OF ALL KINDS OF DEPENDENCE TO THE EAST AND WEST SUPER-POWERS.

2) WE FULLY SUPPORT ALL OPPRESSED NATIONS IN THEIR STRUGGLE TO OBTAIN FREEDOM AND INDEPENDENCE, AND RECALL THEM TO THE VERY FACT THAT THEY MUST ALWAYS FIGHT FOR THEIR OWN RIGHTS, REVOLT AND FIGHT AGAINST ALL SUPER-POWERS TO THE END.

3) I HAVE ALWAYS SAID AND WARNED THAT IF, THE OPPRESSED EAST AND AFRICA DO NOT RELY ON THEIR OWN EFFORTS THEY WILL CONTINUE TO BE EXTORTED AND OPPRESSED FOR EVER.

4) WE SUPPORT THE DEFENCELESS PEOPLE OF PALESTINE AND LEBANON AGAINST ISRAEL.

5) WE FULLY SUPPORT THE BRAVE MOSLEM PEOPLE OF AFGHANISTAN.

6) REMOVE UNDOUBTFULLY ANYBODY IN ANY POSITION WHO INTENDS TO COMPROMISE WITH THE EAST OR WEST BECAUSE ANY SORT OF COMPROMISE WITH THEM IS ALIENATION FROM AND TREASON TO ISLAM AND MOSLEMS.

ISLAMIC REPUBLIC PARTY
INT. SECTION

Ayatollah Ruhollah Khomeini (1902–89)

Ayatollah Khomeini was an Iranian religious and political leader, who, following the 1979 Iranian Revolution, established the world's first Islamic republic in the twentieth century. Born in 1902, he was educated in the holy city of Qom, and became a distinguished religious scholar and an authority on divine law. At first uninvolved in politics, he became a leader of the opposition to the pro-Western regime of the Shah in the early 1960s. Arrested in 1962, he was exiled in 1964, spending the next seventeen years in Turkey, Iraq, and France. It was during this period that he perfected his doctrine of clerical governance, by which the guardianship of the people would be vested in a just and pious 'jurisconsult'. In January 1979 the Shah's government collapsed and Khomeini returned home to a hero's welcome. Following a referendum, he declared Iran an Islamic republic and was himself appointed as supreme religious and political leader for life. During the next decade he established Islamic rule in Iran, maintained a consistently anti-Western stance, and supported many revolutionary movements throughout the world. From 1980 to 1988 he led Iran in the war against Iraq that resulted in many thousands of deaths and ended in a stalemate. His funeral in 1989 was the largest recorded in human history with an estimated eleven million mourners present.

IMAM KHOMEINI, THE LEADER OF THE ISLAMIC
REVOLUTION OF IRAN AND VOICE OF THE
MUSTAZ'AFIN (OPPRESSED) OF THE WORLD.

Pope John Paul II (1920–2005)

One of the longest-serving Popes in history, the first Pole to hold the office, and the first non-Italian since the sixteenth century, John Paul II was a charismatic leader of the Roman Catholic Church who attracted adulation and opposition in almost equal measure. Born Karel Józef Wojtyła in Wadowice, near to Krakow, his formative years were spent during first the Nazi and then the Soviet occupation of his country. He survived the Second World War by working in a stone quarry and a chemical works, and was ordained in 1946. He became a teacher of moral theology and ethics at the universities of Krakow and Lublin, and also became known for his youth work, and his writings, literary as well as theological. Appointed Bishop of Ombi in 1958,

he became Archbishop of Krakow in 1964 and a Cardinal in 1967 while Poland was still under Communist rule. Following the short-lived papacy of John Paul I, in 1978 he was the surprise choice of the College of Cardinals to be the next Pope. John Paul II saw himself as pastor to the world and travelled more widely than any of his predecessors. One of his first visits was to Poland, where he encouraged the growth of the opposition Solidarity movement. The degree to which he was responsible for the eventual fall of Communism in Eastern Europe in 1989 has been disputed. In social matters he was a conservative, maintaining the Church's opposition to all forms of birth control, abortion, euthanasia, and the ordination of women. He also opposed 'liberation theology' in Latin America. He campaigned for social justice and for the relief of debt in the developing world, and opposed the Iraq War. He survived a KGB-sponsored assassination attempt in 1981, but from 1992 onwards his health began to decline. A prolific creator of saints himself, there have been moves since his death for him to be canonized.

Margaret Thatcher (1925–   )

Known by many as the 'Iron Lady', Margaret Thatcher is a formidable politician who became Britain's first female Prime Minister from 1979 to 1990, and the longest continuously serving since the early nineteenth century. The child of a Grantham grocer, she read Chemistry at Somerville College, Oxford, before entering Parliament in 1959. She changed both the economic and the political landscape of Britain, seeing the adoption of tough economic reforms through monetarist policies, the reduction of the power of the trade unions, epitomized by her defeat of the miners' strike of 1984, privatization of state-owned industries, victory in the Falklands War of 1982, and the winning of a substantial rebate from Britain's financial contributions to the European Union. Firmly anti-communist, Mrs Thatcher was a close ally of President Ronald Reagan, supposedly even telling him what he was thinking, but she also famously remarked of Mikhail Gorbachev that he was a man with whom she could do business. Her introduction of the unpopular poll tax for local government, and her strident opposition to further moves towards European integration, eventually led to a revolt by her own MPs, which brought about her resignation. President Mitterrand of France once allegedly described her as having 'the eyes of Caligula and the lips of Marilyn Monroe'. Here she is pictured with the Deputy Prime Minister of Hungary, Jezef Marjai.

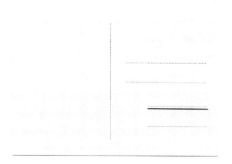

Lech Wałęsa (1943–   )

One of the founders and first leader of Solidarity, the first independent trade union within the Soviet bloc, Wałęsa became a symbol of resistance to Communism, and later was elected as the first post-Communist President of Poland. Wałęsa was an electrician who, in 1970, was a member of an illegal strike committee at the Gdansk shipyard. After the end of the strike he was arrested and spent a year in jail. In 1980 he once again became leader of a strike at the shipyard, which led to the formation of Solidarity. Initially the Polish government appeared unclear how to deal with Solidarity, and for a year the union survived as a rival to the Communist Party. However, in December 1981 General Jaruzelski declared martial law, Solidarity was disbanded and Wałęsa re-arrested. In 1983 he was awarded the Nobel Peace Prize but was not permitted to travel to Oslo to receive it. In 1989 Wałęsa led the Citizenship Committee of a revived Solidarity, which acted as an opposition party in all but name. The opposition won a sweeping victory in parliamentary elections, and further 'round table' discussions led to the peaceful dismantling of the Communist state. Wałęsa was elected President of Poland in 1990 and served until 1995, when he was narrowly defeated in the presidential election. He stood again in 2000 but gained only 1 per cent of the vote. He has received numerous awards and commendations for his human rights activities.

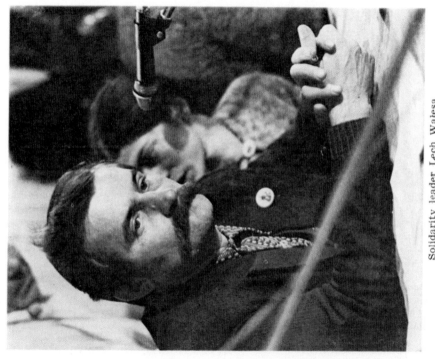

Solidarity leader Lech Wałęsa

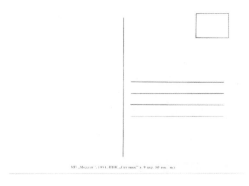

MD „Moscow", 1991, ПЦК „Сувенир" х.9 тир. 50 тыс. экз.

Andrei Sakharov (1921–89)

Sakharov was an eminent Soviet nuclear physicist, who later became a political dissident and human rights activist. In 1948 he participated in the development of the first Soviet atomic bomb, and from 1950 worked on developing the hydrogen bomb. However, during the 1950s he is said to have felt increasingly concerned about the moral and political implications of his work, leading to his removal from work on military projects. In the 1960s he argued for peaceful co-existence between the superpowers, and in 1970 he was one of the founders of the Moscow Human Rights Committee. Awarded the Nobel Peace Prize in 1975, he was not allowed to travel to Oslo to receive it. In 1980, as a result of protesting against the Soviet invasion of Afghanistan, he was sent into internal exile in the closed city of Gorky (now Nizhny Novgorod), only being allowed to return to Moscow in 1986, after Mikhail Gorbachev had come to power. Continuing his campaign for human rights in the Soviet Union, in the more liberal atmosphere of 1989 he was elected to the Soviet parliament, the All-Union Congress of People's Deputies, where he became one of the leaders of the democratic opposition. At the height of his fame and his influence, he died of a sudden heart attack.

АНДРЕЙ САХАРОВ
(1921-1989)

Ronald Reagan (1911–2004) and Mikhail Gorbachev (1931–)

Together, Ronald Reagan and Mikhail Gorbachev were in part responsible for the end of the Cold War and the demise of Communism in Eastern Europe.

A former screen actor, Reagan (left) served as Governor of California before being elected fortieth President of the United States; he served two terms from 1981 to 1989. Known as the 'Great Communicator', Reagan aimed to restore 'the great confident roar of American progress and growth and optimism'. To do this he introduced laissez-faire economic policies that became known as 'Reaganomics'. His foreign policy was characterized by 'peace through strength'. He aimed to outspend the USSR on military defence, not least through his 'Star Wars' programme, but, although calling the Soviet Union an 'evil empire', negotiated with Mikhail Gorbachev on reducing the numbers of nuclear missiles. This twin-pronged strategy is widely regarded as having contributed to the end of the Cold War and subsequent break-up of the Soviet Union, and Reagan remains one of the most popular presidents in American history.

Mikhail Gorbachev (right) came to power in the Soviet Union in 1985, determined to inject new energy into the Soviet political and economic system. He came from a peasant background in Soviet North Caucasus and joined the Communist Party in 1952. His policies of perestroika (restructuring) and glasnost (liberalization or openness) led to an increase in both personal freedom and political pluralism in the Soviet Union and ultimately also to the demise of the USSR itself, as the nationalities question within the Soviet Union re-emerged. Abroad, his summit meetings with presidents Reagan and Bush signalled the end of the Cold War, whilst his policies led to the largely peaceful end of the Communist regimes in Eastern Europe. Overthrown as a result of a failed coup by Communist hardliners in 1991, Gorbachev remains a far more popular person abroad than he does in Russia. He was awarded the Nobel Peace Prize in 1990.

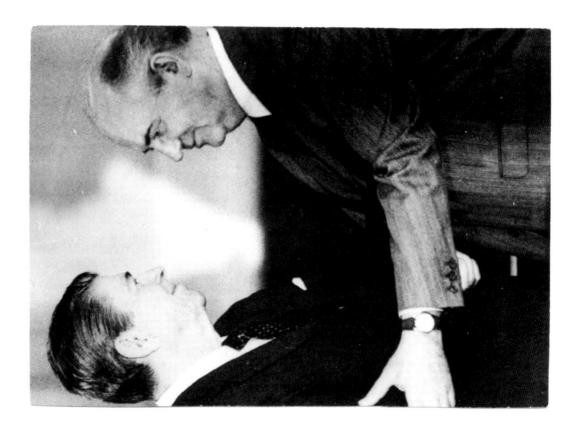

POST CARD

A47 Jafta Cards, Harare, Zimbabwe

WELCOME MANDELA— Zimbabwe, March 1990
Nelson Mandela and Robert Mugabe at Harare Airport
Photograph: Margaret Waller

Nelson Mandela (1918–   ) and Robert Mugabe (1924–   )

Imprisoned for twenty-seven years by the Apartheid government in South Africa, Nelson Mandela (left) was the leading icon of the worldwide Anti-Apartheid Movement. Released in 1990, his policy of reconciliation and negotiation led to the peaceful transition of South Africa into a multiracial democracy, and he served as first President of the new South Africa from 1994 to 1999. He was awarded the Nobel Peace Prize in 1993. Widely seen as a truly inspirational figure with trememdous moral authority, Mandela has become a universal hero.

Robert Mugabe (right) was a hero at the time his country, Zimbabwae (then called Rhodesia) secured its independence from Britain in 1979. An outspoken figure, Mugabe has remained head of state during a period when Zimbabwe, once known as 'the breadbasket of Africa', has become dependent on outside food aid, with political unrest and a record-breaking rate of inflation. He has acquired an increasingly controversial international profile.

Ian Paisley (1926–   )

A powerful orator and minister in the Free Presbyterian Church, which he helped found, for forty years Paisley was the voice of militant Ulster Unionism. Initially a member of the Ulster Unionist Party, he founded his own Democratic Unionist Party, which eventually supplanted the UUP as the main Unionist party in the province. He was also a Westminster MP from 1970. For many years Paisley was known as 'Dr No' on account of his implacable opposition to the aspirations of the Nationalist community of Northern Ireland. He opposed the Sunningdale Agreement (1973), the Anglo-Irish Agreement (1985) and the Good Friday Agreement (1998), as well as supporting the Ulster Workers Council strike (1974) and the Orange Order's standoff at Drumcree (1995). However, near the end of his long career in Irish politics, he surprised many by agreeing to enter a power-sharing administration with Sinn Fein in 2007. He served as First Minister of Northern Ireland until 2008, and established a good relationship with his deputy, Martin McGuinness, to the extent that they became familiarly known as the 'chuckle brothers'.

Gerry Adams (1948–   )

Gerry Adams has been a key member of the Republican movement in Northern Ireland since the 1970s and has served as president of Sinn Fein since 1983. Although regarded by some sections of the Unionist community as little more than a terrorist, he is reported to have told the Republican movement as early as 1979 that victory could not be achieved by military means alone. This led to the strategy of the 'Armalite and the ballot box', and Adams persuaded his party to take up seats both in the Irish Dail and later in the Northern Ireland Assembly, both moves representing major shifts in policy. He has been a Westminster MP from 1983 to 1992 and since 1997. He played a major role in the series of talks that paved the way for a democratically negotiated peace settlement in Northern Ireland, which has seen an end to the so-called Troubles and the participation of Sinn Fein in a power-sharing administration.

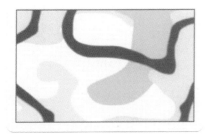

Saddam Hussein (1937–2006)

The President of Iraq from 1979 to 2003, Saddam Hussein was feared by many for the violence and ruthlessness of his rule, but was a hero to others for standing up to both Israel and the West. A secular exponent of Pan-Arabism, he saw himself as the heir to Nasser and a modernizer. He joined the secularist Ba'ath Party whilst a student and in 1959 participated in an unsuccessful coup against the government. He fled abroad but returned in 1963, when he was imprisoned. He escaped in 1967 and the following year took part in the coup that brought the Ba'th Party to power. Initially the power behind the throne, he became President in 1979. In 1980 he took Iraq into an eight-year war with Iran that ended in stalemate and ravaged the economies of both countries, and in 1990 he invaded Kuwait, thus precipitating the First Gulf War. After suffering defeat at the hands of a UN-authorized international coalition, Saddam managed to retain power and suppressed the Shi'ite and Kurdish communities who had risen in revolt at the end of the war. Claiming that Saddam had weapons of mass destruction ready to be deployed against the West, the USA launched a war against Iraq in 2003. After a lengthy search in which a deck of 'wanted persons' playing cards, of which this is one, was used to identify Saddamists, Saddam was captured, tried in Baghdad, and executed on 30 December 2006.

A ♠

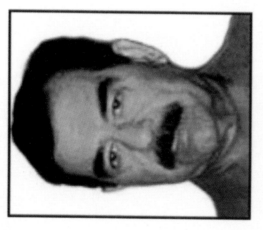

SADDAM HUSAYN AL-TIKRITI
President

A ♠

Tenzin Gyatso, Fourteenth Dalai Lama (1935–)

The Dalai Lama is widely considered to be the spiritual and temporal leader of the Tibetan people, and a reincarnation of a line of Buddhist teachers that stretches back to the sixteenth century. The present Dalai Lama, Tenzin Gyatso, was born to a family of farmers in 1935. Two years later he was proclaimed to be the reincarnation of the thirteenth Dalai Lama, and in 1950 he was enthroned in Lhasa. This happened as the Chinese army was in the process of invading Tibet, and the first task of the new ruler was to seek some accommodation with the Chinese Communist government. The Dalai Lama travelled to Beijing where in 1951 he agreed to the Seventeen Point Agreement for the Peaceful Liberation of Tibet, which proclaimed Chinese sovereignty over Tibet, whilst allowing some degree of local autonomy. In 1959 he was forced to flee to India following the failure of the Tibetan uprising. Since then the Dalai Lama has been based in Dharamsala, where he heads the Tibetan Government in Exile. He has continued to press for the resolution of the Tibetan situation by peaceful means, and in 1989 was awarded the Nobel Peace Prize in recognition of his efforts. In 2008 when unrest broke out again in Lhasa he called for calm, but also condemned the Chinese for their violent response to the Tibetan protests. An inspirational figure to many, the present Dalai Lama has been the first to travel to the West and spread his version of Buddhism with its doctrine of peace, compassion, and harmony to a worldwide audience.

'Choose Freedom ', from The Burma Campaign UK
Broughton House, 6/8 - 21 Broughton Road, London HW9 5JT
telephone 00 44 20 7281 7377 fax 00 44 20 7272 3559
www.burmacampaign.org.uk

Aung San Suu Kyi (1945–)

Currently (2008) under house arrest for the sixth
successive year, Aung San Suu Kyi is the leader of the
Burmese National League for Democracy. The daughter
of General Aung San, the Burmese nationalist leader
who led the fight for independence from Britain, she
was brought up partly in India, and was educated at St
Hugh's College, Oxford, where she met her husband,
the academic Michael Aris. Returning to Burma in 1988
she became the leader of the pro-democracy movement
which won 82 per cent of the vote in the elections that
took place in 1990. However, the military regime refused
to give up power and she was placed under house arrest
that lasted until 1995. Inspired by Gandhi and Martin
Luther King, she has consistently campaigned for peaceful
democratic reforms and change through dialogue, and
in 1991 she was awarded the Nobel Peace Prize. She
was again placed under house arrest from 2000 to
2002, when she was released after secret talks with the
Burmese generals. However, she was re-arrested in 2003
and has remained under house arrest ever since. She is
regarded by many, like Nelson Mandela, as both a beacon
of hope to her people that democracy can be achieved in
Burma, and a symbol worldwide of steadfast and peaceful
resistance in the face of oppression. The following is
attributed to her: 'It is not power that corrupts but fear.
Fear of losing power corrupts those who wield it and
fear of the scourge of power corrupts those who are
subject to it.'

WHISPERING FREEDOM
Choose Freedom / Join The Burma Campaign UK